Get Over Yourself and Get It Done

Jacob Jones

Get Over Yourself and Get It Done
© 2024 Jacob Jones
All rights reserved.

Jacob Jones
North York, Ontario, Canada

This book is a work of nonfiction. While the author has made every effort to ensure the accuracy of the information herein, the author and publisher assume no responsibility for errors, inaccuracies, omissions, or any outcomes related to the use of this book. Any perceived slight of specific people, organizations, or groups is unintentional.

ISBN: 978-1-300-75514-2
Cover Design by: Jacob Jones
Edited by: Jacob Jones
Printed in Canada

First Edition: 2024

Preface: No One's Coming to Save You

Let me tell you a story. It's not the kind of story with a happy ending—or any ending, really. It's the story of the person you are right now, sitting with this book in your hands, reading these words. It's a story of potential, excuses, fear, ambition, failure, and hope. And like every story, it has a turning point. That's where we are right now—this moment, right here.

I don't know why you picked up this book. Maybe you're tired of feeling stuck. Maybe you're pissed off at yourself for not being where you thought you'd be by now. Maybe you're looking for a spark, a guide, or some permission to get moving. Whatever it is, here's what I know: you're here because you want more. You might not say it out loud, but deep down, you know you're capable of more. And maybe that terrifies you. Good. That means you're in the right place.

This book isn't here to make you feel good. It's not here to tell you that you're fine just the way you are or that the universe will magically align to hand you your dreams. That's not how life works. You're not fine. If you were, you wouldn't need this book. And the universe? It doesn't give a damn about your plans. If you want something, you're going to have to work for it, fight for it, and take responsibility for it.

The truth is, no one's coming to save you. That realization can either break you or set you free. It broke me at first. For years, I waited for the perfect opportunity, the right person, the magical moment when everything would fall into place. Spoiler alert: it never came. One day, I realized the only thing standing between me and the life I wanted was me. My excuses. My fears. My laziness. My obsession with what other people thought.

It wasn't an easy truth to swallow, but it was the most important one. Because once I accepted that I was the problem, I also realized I was the solution. And that changed everything.

This book isn't going to hold your hand. It's not going to coddle you or tell you that it's okay to keep waiting, keep overthinking, or keep playing small. It's here to wake you up, shake you up, and piss you off if that's what it takes to get you moving. You don't need more inspiration. You need action. You don't need another excuse. You need ownership. And you don't need someone else to save you. You need to save yourself.

Every chapter in this book is a challenge. A slap in the face when you need it. A kick in the ass when you're dragging your feet. If you're looking for a feel-good, soft-and-fluffy self-help book, this isn't it. But if you're ready to be honest with yourself, to take responsibility for your life, and to do the hard, ugly, unglamorous work of building the life you want—then keep reading.

This book isn't here to solve your problems. It's here to remind you that you're the only one who can. And if that doesn't sit well with you, good. That discomfort is where growth begins. The choice is yours. Always has been. Always will be.

Warning: This Book Will Offend You

Let's get something straight before you read another word: this book isn't here to coddle you. It's not here to stroke your ego, validate your excuses, or make you feel warm and fuzzy about where you are right now. It's here to wake you up. And waking up is never comfortable.

You're going to get called out. You're going to feel attacked. You're going to come face-to-face with truths you've been avoiding, excuses you've been making, and habits that are holding you back. If you're not ready for that, close this book now and go back to whatever comfortable mediocrity you've been settling for. Seriously, I won't be offended. This book isn't for everyone.

But if you're still here, then you're exactly the kind of person this book is for. The person who knows they're capable of more but hasn't figured out how to get out of their own way. The person who's tired of spinning their wheels and making excuses. The person who's ready to hear the truth—even if it hurts.

This book is a mirror, not a handout. It's going to show you who you are, where you're falling short, and what you need to do to change. And let me tell you now: it's not going to be easy. If you're expecting a quick fix or some magical, feel-good life hack, you're in for a rude awakening. Growth is hard. Progress is painful. But it's worth it—if you're willing to do the work.

So, here's the deal: if you're not ready to take responsibility for your life, put this book down. If you're not willing to face your fears, challenge your excuses, and take action, save yourself the trouble and walk away now. But if you're ready—truly ready—to stop bullshitting yourself and start building the life you want, then buckle up. It's time to get real.

You've been warned. Now let's get started.

Chapter 1: Stop Overthinking: You're Not That Special

Let's rip the Band-Aid off quickly: most of what's holding you back is in your head, and it's nonsense. Overthinking isn't intelligence or preparation—it's a slow, self-imposed death. It's a trap disguised as caution, and it's keeping you stuck while everyone else speeds past. Here's the truth: your brain is lying to you, constantly, and if you keep believing it, you'll end up wasting your life playing mental ping-pong while others build empires.

We've all done it: you've got an idea, a goal, or a plan. But instead of taking the first step, you sit there spinning your wheels. You run through every possible scenario, anticipate every potential disaster, and create imaginary problems to solve before they even exist. The result? You convince yourself to wait. "Just one more day," you say. "I'll start when I'm ready." Guess what? You'll never be ready. You'll just keep sitting there, chewing on the same thoughts, while the world keeps moving.

Here's the kicker: you're not that special. Yeah, I said it. Let it sting for a second. It's not meant to insult you; it's meant to free you. Your problems?

They're not unique. Your fears? Everyone's got them. That little voice in your head telling you that you're not good enough or that you're destined to fail? It's not some profound truth—it's just the same old crap everyone deals with. The difference is, successful people don't listen to it.

Think of the most successful person you know. The kind of person who seems like they've got it all figured out. You think they've never doubted themselves? Of course, they have. But they didn't sit there marinating in their doubts. They moved forward anyway. You're not going to think your way into success. You're going to act your way into it. Overthinking is procrastination in a fancy suit. The sooner you realize that, the sooner you'll start making progress.

Let me tell you about a guy I knew—let's call him Mike. Mike had a million ideas. Every time you talked to him, he'd tell you about his "big plans." He was going to start a business, write a book, run a marathon—you name it. But every time I asked him how it was going, he'd give me the same excuse: "I'm still working out the details." The details, he said. For years, Mike stayed "working out the details." You know what he ended up doing? Absolutely nothing. He thought himself into a standstill. His plans never left his head. Don't be a Mike.

The biggest mistake overthinkers make is believing that every decision has to be perfect. Spoiler alert: perfection doesn't exist. The people waiting for the perfect moment or the perfect plan are the same people still waiting when the train leaves the station. Look, the perfect time is now, because now is the only time you're guaranteed. Stop acting like you've got all the time in the world. Time isn't loyal—it won't wait for you. The clock is ticking, and every second you spend overanalyzing is a second you're not getting back.

Let's talk about fear for a second because that's what's really driving all this overthinking. You're scared. Scared of failing, scared of looking stupid, scared of wasting your time. I get it. Fear's a bitch. But here's the thing: fear doesn't go away. It doesn't get smaller just because you're sitting there trying to outsmart it. The only way to make fear irrelevant is to act in spite of it. Action shrinks fear. Inaction feeds it. So, what's it going to be?

And let's get one thing straight: you don't need a roadmap to start. Successful people don't wait for a 100% foolproof plan before taking action. They jump in, make mistakes, and figure it out as they go. You don't need to see the whole staircase to take the first step. Stop worrying about step five when you haven't even taken step one. Thinking won't build the staircase. Action will.

Here's a practical example: say you want to start a business. Your overthinking brain will tell you to research every single detail first—market trends, competition, pricing strategies, the best logo colors. You'll spend months, maybe years, stuck in analysis paralysis. Meanwhile, someone else with half your knowledge but twice your guts has already launched and learned more in three months than you did in three years of thinking. That's the power of action. It beats thinking every time.

Now let's talk about the "what ifs." What if it doesn't work? What if I fail? What if people judge me? You want to know the answer? It doesn't matter. You're going to screw up. That's guaranteed. But every screw-up is a lesson you can't learn by sitting on the sidelines. Failure isn't fatal—it's feedback. And feedback is how you grow. So, stop treating failure like it's the end of the world and start seeing it for what it is: proof that you're trying.

Here's your homework: pick one thing you've been overthinking. Maybe it's a phone call you've been avoiding, a project you've been putting off, or a dream you've been too scared to start. Got it? Good. Now go do it. Not tomorrow. Not next week. Right now. And don't worry about doing it perfectly. Do it badly, if you have to. The point is to act, not analyze. Action is messy, but it's progress. Overthinking is clean, but it's a dead end.

The bottom line is this: overthinking will kill your momentum. It will keep you small. If you want to do something great—hell, if you just want to do something—you've got to get out of your own head. You don't need more time to think. You don't need anyone's permission. You just need to move. So, stop overthinking. Start doing. And don't look back.

Chapter 2: Hard Work Is Ugly, And That's Beautiful

Here's a lie you've been sold: hard work is supposed to look inspiring. Social media is full of influencers posting their "grind," with perfect lighting and a filter, making it look glamorous. But here's the truth no one wants to talk about: real hard work is messy, boring, and downright ugly. It's the sweat-stained, unshowered, bleary-eyed grind that nobody's snapping selfies of. And that's the beauty of it—it's raw, real, and the only thing that gets results.

The world is full of people who think they're working hard. You know the type: they love to tell you how busy they are, how many hours they're putting in, and how much they "hustle." But when you look closer, you realize they're just spinning their wheels. They're busy without being productive. They're working hard at looking like they're working hard. Meanwhile, the real grinders? They're too busy actually doing the work to talk about it.

Hard work isn't sexy, and it's not supposed to be. It's late nights and early mornings. It's saying no to Netflix because you've got a deadline to hit. It's staring at a blank page, a blinking cursor, or a project that's kicking your ass and refusing to give up. It's failing over and over and showing up again anyway. The sooner you embrace the ugliness of the process, the sooner you'll start getting somewhere.

Think about this: have you ever seen a professional athlete train? Not the highlight reels, but the actual training? It's brutal. It's sweat, gritted teeth, and exhaustion. Nobody's out there looking graceful during their fifth set of deadlifts or their eighth lap around the track. But that's what it takes to win. It's the same in everything—whether you're building a business, writing a book, or chasing a dream. If it doesn't feel a little bit like torture sometimes, you're not working hard enough.

Let me tell you about Sarah. Sarah wanted to start her own business—a bakery. She had the recipes, the vision, the whole Pinterest board aesthetic ready to go. But she didn't expect the grind that came with it. She thought it would be all Instagram-worthy cakes and happy customers. What she got instead? 14-hour days covered in flour, burned fingers, bills piling up, and weeks where she didn't know if she'd break even. But she stuck with it. She didn't quit when it got ugly, and now her bakery is thriving. Why? Because she didn't let the hard, unglamorous work scare her off. She embraced it.

Here's the problem: too many people quit when the work gets ugly. The second it stops being fun or easy, they're out. But here's the thing: the ugliness is part of the process. It's where you learn, grow, and earn your success. Anyone can work hard when it's fun. The real test is whether you can keep going when it sucks.

Now, let's talk about the mindset you need to push through the grind. First, stop looking for shortcuts. They don't exist. If you're spending more time trying to hack your way to success than actually doing the work, you're wasting your energy. Hard work is the only hack you need. Second, stop comparing your journey to someone else's highlight reel. You're seeing the polished end result, not the blood, sweat, and tears it took to get there. Your journey is yours—own it.

Here's a little exercise for you: think about something you've achieved that you're proud of. Got it? Now, think about the work it took to get there. I bet it wasn't pretty. Maybe it was late nights studying, extra hours at the office, or countless failures before you got it right. But you pushed through. That's what hard work is: doing the ugly stuff because you know the payoff is worth it.

And let's not forget one of the most important truths about hard work: no one is going to do it for you. You're not entitled to success, and you're not going to stumble into it by accident. If you want it, you have to earn it. Period. That means showing up every day, putting in the effort, and grinding it out—even when you don't feel like it. Especially when you don't feel like it.

Look, I'm not here to sugarcoat it. Hard work sucks. It's uncomfortable, exhausting, and sometimes downright miserable. But it's also the most rewarding thing you'll ever do. Because at the end of the day, the ugly grind is what separates the dreamers from the doers. It's the difference between wishing for success and actually achieving it.

So, here's your challenge: embrace the ugly. Stop looking for inspiration or motivation to strike. Those are fair-weather friends. Instead, commit to showing up and doing the work, no matter how messy it gets. Because the grind? That's where the magic happens.

Chapter 3: No One Owes You Shit (Not Even Your Dreams)

Here's a reality check you probably don't want to hear: no one owes you anything. Not success, not happiness, not even a pat on the back for your effort. The world isn't sitting around waiting to hand you a gold star because you tried really hard. It doesn't care how badly you want something or how much you think you deserve it. Success isn't a gift—it's something you take by putting in the work, day after day, without expecting applause.

Somewhere along the way, a lot of us got this idea that life is supposed to be fair. That if you show up, put in a little effort, and follow the rules, you'll get what you want. Hate to break it to you, but fair is a fantasy. Life doesn't hand out participation trophies. It rewards action, persistence, and grit. If you're sitting around waiting for someone to notice your potential and give you a shot, you'll be waiting forever.

Think about it: how often do you find yourself saying, "I deserve this"? Maybe it's a promotion at work, recognition for your talents, or a break from the grind. The truth is, you don't deserve shit just for existing. Harsh? Maybe. True? Absolutely. The only thing you're entitled to is the opportunity to work for what you want. Everything else is earned.

Let's get one thing straight: the world isn't out to get you. It's not some evil, sentient force conspiring to keep you down. It's just indifferent. That might sound depressing, but it's actually liberating. It means your success—or failure—isn't determined by some cosmic sense of justice. It's determined by what you do. That's power in its purest form. It means you're in control, whether you like it or not.

Stop waiting for someone to save you. Stop waiting for someone to notice your potential, hand you a raise, or tell you you're good enough. It's not going to happen. You've got to step up and take what's yours. That means asking for the raise, even if it scares the hell out of you. It means putting your work out there, even if you're terrified of rejection. It means showing up and proving yourself every single day, even when no one's watching.

The problem is, too many people treat hard work like a transaction. They think if they put in X amount of effort, they're guaranteed Y amount of success. But that's not how it works. You can do everything right and still fail. You can work your ass off and still fall short. And when that happens, you've got two choices: you can whine about how unfair it is, or you can get back to work. Guess which one actually gets you somewhere?

Here's the brutal truth: the world doesn't care about your dreams. It doesn't care how much potential you have or how badly you want something. It only cares about results. That's not to say your dreams don't matter—they do. But they only matter to *you*. It's your job to protect them, nurture them, and fight like hell to make them happen. No one else is going to do that for you.

And let's talk about failure for a second because it's inevitable. You're going to fail. Probably a lot. And when you do, the world isn't going to feel sorry for you. It's not going to pat you on the back and tell you to try again. It's just going to keep moving, indifferent to your struggle. That might sound cold, but it's actually freeing. Failure isn't a judgment—it's just feedback. It's a reminder that you're in the arena, that you're trying, and that you're learning. But it's up to you to pick yourself up and keep going.

No one owes you success, but here's the good news: you don't owe the world an explanation, either. You don't have to justify your ambitions or apologize for wanting more. You don't have to wait for permission to chase your goals. The only approval you need is your own. So stop looking for validation from people who don't matter and start betting on yourself.

The sooner you accept that the world doesn't owe you anything, the sooner you can stop waiting and start building. Because at the end of the day, no one's coming to save you. No one's going to hand you your dreams on a silver platter. If you want something, you've got to fight for it. Relentlessly. Unapologetically. Without expecting a damn thing in return.

So, what are you waiting for? Stop hoping for life to play fair. Stop wishing for handouts. Put your head down, do the work, and earn it. Because no one owes you shit—but that's what makes it so much sweeter when you succeed.

Chapter 4: Failure Is Your Best Friend (And You're Stuck with It)

Let's talk about failure. Everyone's terrified of it, and yet it's the one thing you're guaranteed to meet if you're doing anything worth a damn. Here's the uncomfortable truth: failure isn't your enemy—it's your ride-or-die. It's the ugly, stubborn best friend you didn't ask for but can't live without. And the sooner you learn to embrace it, the better off you'll be.

Think about it: when was the last time you failed at something? Be honest. Did you take it personally? Did you throw yourself a little pity party? Most people do. Failure has a way of making you feel like the universe is pointing and laughing at you. But that's not failure's job. Failure isn't there to humiliate you; it's there to teach you. Every time you screw up, you're handed a free lesson—no tuition required. The only cost is your pride.

The problem is, most people don't see failure as feedback. They see it as a verdict. They take it as proof that they're not good enough, smart enough, or capable enough. So, they give up. They retreat to their comfort zones, tell themselves they're not cut out for it, and never try again. But here's the truth: failure isn't telling you to stop. It's telling you to adjust, to tweak your approach, to try again with more information.

You've heard the clichés: "Fail fast," "Fail forward," "Failure is a stepping stone to success." Yeah, yeah, we've all rolled our eyes at those platitudes. But the thing about clichés is they're rooted in truth. Failure is inevitable, but it's also invaluable. Every time you fail, you're collecting data. You're learning what doesn't work, which gets you closer to figuring out what does. No failure, no growth—it's that simple.

Here's the thing about success: it's built on a mountain of failures. You don't get to skip the hard parts. You don't get to succeed without stumbling along the way. Show me someone who's never failed, and I'll show you someone who's never tried anything meaningful. Failure isn't a sign that you're on the wrong path; it's a sign that you're in the game.

Look at some of the greatest successes in history. Michael Jordan didn't make his high school varsity basketball team. Walt Disney was fired from a newspaper job because he "lacked imagination." Oprah was told she wasn't fit for television. Did they let those failures define them? Hell no. They used them as fuel. They got back up, tried again, and proved everyone wrong. You can, too—if you're willing to embrace failure instead of running from it.

But let's get one thing straight: failure doesn't feel good. It stings. It bruises your ego. It makes you want to crawl under a rock and stay there. And that's okay. No one's asking you to pretend it doesn't suck. The goal isn't to enjoy failure—it's to endure it. To push through the discomfort and come out stronger on the other side.

So, how do you do that? How do you turn failure into your best friend instead of your worst enemy? First, you have to change the way you think about it. Stop seeing failure as the opposite of success and start seeing it as a part of the process. Success isn't a straight line; it's a squiggly, messy, back-and-forth journey. Failure is just one of the stops along the way.

Second, stop taking failure personally. It's not about you—it's about the approach you tried. If something didn't work, it doesn't mean you suck; it means that particular strategy sucked. Separate your self-worth from your performance. You're not your failures, and you're not your successes, either. You're just a person figuring it out like everyone else.

Third, learn to laugh at yourself. Seriously. Nothing takes the power out of failure like a good sense of humor. Did you bomb a presentation? Laugh at how awkward it was and move on. Did you start a side hustle that flopped? Joke about how you're now the proud owner of 500 unsellable widgets. Humor turns failure from a tragedy into a comedy, and trust me, life is a lot easier when you stop taking yourself so damn seriously.

Finally, and most importantly, keep going. Failure only beats you if you let it. The people who succeed aren't the ones who never fail; they're the ones who refuse to quit. They're the ones who fall down ten times and get up eleven. It's not about avoiding failure—it's about being relentless in the face of it.

Here's the bottom line: failure isn't optional, but quitting is. You're going to screw up. You're going to faceplant. You're going to have moments where you wonder if it's all worth it. And when that happens, you have a choice: let failure define you, or let it refine you. The choice is yours.

So, stop running from failure and start running toward it. Make it your ally, your mentor, your constant companion. Because failure isn't the enemy of success—it's the foundation of it. And if

you can learn to see it that way, there's nothing
you can't achieve.

Chapter 5: The Grind: If It Feels Good, You're Doing It Wrong

Let's get something straight: the grind isn't supposed to feel good. If it does, you're not really grinding. The grind is uncomfortable. It's grueling. It's that thing no one likes to talk about because it's not pretty or glamorous. It's the unsexy, thankless work that happens in the shadows while the rest of the world is out having fun.

Everyone loves the idea of success, but very few people are willing to embrace the grind that makes it possible. You think successful people wake up every day thrilled to push themselves to the limit? Hell no. They wake up tired, unmotivated, and sometimes even miserable—just like you do. The difference is, they do it anyway. Because they know the grind is where the magic happens.

The grind isn't about inspiration. It's not about feeling motivated or chasing some fleeting high. It's about discipline. It's about showing up when you don't want to, pushing through when you're exhausted, and giving it your all even when no one's watching. It's about doing the hard, boring, repetitive work that builds the foundation for success.

And let's be real: the grind will test you. It'll make you question why you started in the first place. It'll make you want to quit a thousand times over. But that's the point. The grind isn't just about achieving a goal—it's about proving to yourself that you have what it takes to stick with it when things get tough. It's about building resilience, one hard-earned step at a time.

Here's where most people get it wrong: they think the grind is a phase. They think it's something you push through for a little while until you "make it," and then life magically gets easier. Newsflash: the grind never ends. It just evolves. If you're doing it right, every level of success comes with new challenges, new obstacles, and new reasons to grind even harder. The goal isn't to escape the grind—it's to embrace it.

Look at the greats in any field—athletes, artists, entrepreneurs, you name it. They didn't get where they are by accident. They didn't luck their way to the top. They got there by grinding day in and day out, even when they didn't feel like it. Michael Phelps didn't become the most decorated Olympian of all time by skipping swim practice because he was tired. Beyoncé didn't build her empire by calling it a day when she was "kinda over it." They showed up. They put in the work. They embraced the grind.

But let's not sugarcoat it: the grind sucks. It's early mornings and late nights. It's missing out on happy hours, weekends, and sometimes even sleep. It's doing the same thing over and over until it feels like your brain might explode. It's the part no one likes to talk about because it's not fun or exciting. But it's also the part that separates the dreamers from the doers.

The grind isn't glamorous, but it's necessary. You can't shortcut your way to success. You can't outsmart the grind, outsource it, or wish it away. You have to do the work, plain and simple. And the sooner you accept that, the sooner you'll start making real progress.

Here's the truth: if you're comfortable, you're not grinding. Growth doesn't happen in your comfort zone. It happens when you're uncomfortable, stretched thin, and on the verge of giving up. That's where you find out what you're really made of. That's where you build the skills, the resilience, and the grit you need to succeed.

So, how do you embrace the grind? First, stop romanticizing the end result. Success isn't some magical destination where all your problems disappear. It's a journey—a long, hard, often frustrating journey. And the grind is the vehicle that gets you there. If you can learn to love the process, even when it sucks, you've already won half the battle.

Second, stop waiting for motivation. Motivation is a fair-weather friend. It's there when things are easy, but it's nowhere to be found when the grind gets tough. Discipline, on the other hand, sticks with you. Discipline is showing up when you're tired, pushing through when you're frustrated, and doing the work even when you'd rather be doing anything else. Discipline is what keeps you going when motivation bails on you.

Third, embrace the suck. Seriously. Stop trying to make the grind easier and start leaning into the discomfort. The harder it is, the more it's teaching you. The more you want to quit, the more you're growing. Pain is temporary, but the rewards of pushing through are permanent.

The grind isn't supposed to feel good, but that's what makes it so rewarding. It's the struggle that makes the victory sweeter. It's the sacrifices that make the success meaningful. If it were easy, everyone would do it. But it's not easy—it's hard as hell. And that's why it's worth it.

So, the next time you find yourself dreading the grind, remind yourself why you're doing it. Remind yourself that every drop of sweat, every ounce of effort, and every sacrifice you make is bringing you closer to your goals. And then get back to work. Because if it feels good, you're doing it wrong.

Chapter 6: Excuses Are Just Polished Lies

Let's be clear: excuses are bullshit. And before you start mentally defending yours, let's call them what they really are—polished, dressed-up lies you tell yourself to feel better about not doing the work. They're the justifications you cling to when you're scared, lazy, or unwilling to take responsibility. And the worst part? You've probably convinced yourself they're valid.

Excuses are seductive. They whisper sweet nothings in your ear, convincing you that it's okay to quit, to wait, or to stay exactly where you are. "I don't have the time." "I'm not ready." "It's too risky." These are classic hits on the excuse mixtape, and they've been holding people back for generations. The problem isn't that you don't have time or that you're not ready. The problem is you're choosing not to make the time or get ready.

Here's a harsh truth: everyone has the same 24 hours in a day. The difference between people who succeed and people who don't isn't time—it's priorities. If something matters to you, you'll find a way to make it happen. If it doesn't, you'll find an excuse. It's that simple. Saying you don't have time is just another way of saying it's not important enough to you. And that's fine—just own it. But stop lying to yourself about why you're not where you want to be.

Think about it: when was the last time an excuse actually helped you? Did "I'll start tomorrow" ever build a business? Did "I don't have the resources" ever write a book or launch a career? No. Excuses don't move you forward. They keep you stuck. They're like comfort food for your ego—temporarily satisfying but ultimately unhealthy.

The Anatomy of an Excuse

Let's dissect an excuse for a second. At its core, every excuse is a shield—a way to protect yourself from discomfort, failure, or judgment. When you say, "I don't have enough experience," what you're really saying is, "I'm scared of looking stupid." When you say, "It's not the right time," what you mean is, "I'm afraid to take the leap." Excuses are rooted in fear, and fear is the enemy of progress.

But here's the thing: fear isn't going anywhere. It's always going to be there, lurking in the background, waiting for a chance to derail you. The key isn't to eliminate fear; it's to stop letting it drive the bus. Excuses are just fear in disguise, and the moment you recognize that, they lose their power.

Excuses vs. Reasons

Now, let's clear up a common misconception: there's a difference between excuses and legitimate reasons. If your car breaks down and you're late to work, that's a reason. If you oversleep because you stayed up binge-watching Netflix, that's an excuse. Reasons are external; excuses are internal. Reasons are things you can't control; excuses are things you don't want to control.

The problem is, we're great at turning excuses into reasons in our heads. We twist reality to make ourselves feel better about slacking off. "I didn't go to the gym because I was tired" sounds a lot better than "I didn't go to the gym because I didn't feel like it." But deep down, you know the difference. You can lie to everyone else, but you can't lie to yourself.

Stop Feeding the Excuse Machine

The first step to killing your excuses is to call them out. Be brutally honest with yourself. When you catch yourself making an excuse, ask: "Is this a legitimate obstacle, or am I just avoiding the hard stuff?" Most of the time, you'll realize it's the latter. And that's good news because it means the power to change is in your hands.

The next step? Take ownership. Stop blaming your circumstances, your past, or other people for why you're not where you want to be. You're not a victim of your life—you're the author of it. Every time you make an excuse, you're handing over your pen and letting someone else write your story. Take it back.

And let's address the most common excuse of all: "I'm not ready." Here's the truth: you're never going to feel ready. Readiness is a myth. No one feels 100% prepared for their first big leap, whether it's starting a business, switching careers, or chasing a dream. The only way to get ready is to start. Action creates momentum, and momentum builds confidence. Waiting for readiness is just another excuse to stay in your comfort zone.

The Cost of Excuses

Excuses don't just cost you time—they cost you opportunities. Every time you choose an excuse over action, you're missing a chance to grow, to learn, and to move closer to your goals. And those missed opportunities add up. Before you know it, you've spent years standing still while others have passed you by.

Think about where you want to be a year from now. What does that version of you look like? What have they accomplished? Now, ask yourself this: are your excuses helping you get there? Or are they holding you back? The answer is obvious, but it's not enough to know it—you have to act on it.

No More Excuses

Here's the bottom line: excuses are optional. You don't have to make them. You don't have to let them define you. The next time you catch yourself reaching for one, stop and ask yourself: "What's the truth here?" Be honest, even if it's uncomfortable. And then, instead of making the excuse, make a plan.

It's not going to be easy. Breaking the excuse habit takes effort, self-awareness, and a willingness to own your shit. But the rewards are worth it. Because once you stop making excuses, there's nothing standing between you and what you want. And that's a powerful place to be.

So, no more excuses. No more polished lies. It's time to take ownership of your life and start doing the work. The grind is waiting. Are you ready to show up?

Chapter 7: Passion Won't Save You, Discipline Will

Passion gets all the glory, doesn't it? People love to talk about how passionate they are about their dreams, their goals, their side hustles. "Follow your passion," they say. It sounds so romantic, doesn't it? Like all you need is a burning desire, and the universe will magically align to make your dreams come true. But here's the cold, hard truth: passion isn't enough. It's not even close. Passion might light the fire, but discipline is what keeps it burning.

The problem with passion is it's fickle. It's there when everything's exciting and new, but the second the grind gets tough, passion runs for the hills. It doesn't stick around when you're exhausted, frustrated, or bored. Discipline, though? Discipline is your ride-or-die. It's there when passion flakes out. It's the steady hand that keeps you moving forward, even when you'd rather be doing anything else.

Here's the thing: passion feels good. It's thrilling. It gives you that rush of adrenaline that makes you feel unstoppable. But feelings don't last. They're fleeting, like a sugar high. Discipline, on the other hand, doesn't care how you feel. It shows up every day, rain or shine, ready to get shit done. And that's what separates the dreamers from the doers.

Think about it: how many people do you know who are passionate about something but never seem to make progress? They're always talking about what they're going to do someday, but someday never comes. That's because passion doesn't translate to action without discipline. Passion might get you started, but discipline is what keeps you going. It's the engine that drives the car while passion is just the flashy paint job.

Discipline is doing the work even when you don't feel like it. It's sticking to your commitments when the excitement fades. It's dragging yourself out of bed at 5 a.m. to hit the gym, even when you'd rather sleep in. It's sitting down to write, to study, to grind, even when you're not in the mood. Discipline isn't sexy, but it's effective. And it's the only thing that guarantees progress.

The truth is, discipline is what builds confidence, not passion. Every time you follow through on a commitment, you're proving to yourself that you can rely on yourself. You're building trust in your own ability to show up and do the work. That trust is what gives you the confidence to tackle bigger challenges. Passion doesn't do that. Discipline does.

So, how do you build discipline? You start by making small promises to yourself and keeping them. Get up when you say you're going to get up. Finish the project you've been putting off. Stick to the workout plan, even if you're tired. Every time you keep a promise to yourself, you're reinforcing the habit of discipline. And over time, it becomes second nature.

Of course, discipline isn't easy. It requires sacrifice. It means choosing long-term gains over short-term pleasure. It means saying no to distractions, no to excuses, and sometimes even no to things you enjoy. But the payoff is worth it. Because while passion might get you halfway there, discipline will take you all the way.

Let me be clear: I'm not saying passion is worthless. It's not. Passion is important—it's what gives you a sense of purpose and direction. But it's not a substitute for discipline. Passion is the why, but discipline is the how. You need both. Without passion, discipline becomes a grind without meaning. But without discipline, passion is just a pipe dream.

The problem is, too many people lean on passion as a crutch. They think, "If I'm passionate enough, it'll work out." Wrong. Passion doesn't write the book, build the business, or finish the marathon. Passion is a spark, but discipline is the fuel. And without fuel, the spark dies out.

So, the next time you're tempted to lean on passion alone, remind yourself: passion won't save you. It won't push you through the hard days or carry you across the finish line. Discipline will. Passion might feel good, but discipline gets results. And at the end of the day, results are what matter.

You don't need to feel inspired to get started. You don't need to feel motivated to keep going. All you need is the discipline to show up, day after day, and do the work. Passion can join you if it wants, but if it doesn't, who cares? You've got discipline. And discipline doesn't quit.

Chapter 8: How to Shut Up and Get Started

Let's cut the crap: you're probably overcomplicating things. You've got all these big plans in your head, ideas for what you're going to do, and you're just waiting for the right moment. But the right moment doesn't exist, and your plans don't mean a damn thing until you do something about them. The biggest obstacle between you and your goals is simple—you haven't started yet.

Why? Because starting is scary. Starting means stepping into the unknown, risking failure, and putting yourself out there. It's way easier to sit around and "plan." To research. To "get inspired." To tell yourself you're waiting for everything to line up perfectly. Spoiler alert: perfection is a myth. The stars will never align. The universe doesn't owe you a green light. If you want to make something happen, you have to make the first move.

The truth is, starting isn't about being ready. It's about deciding. Deciding that today is the day you stop making excuses and start taking action. Deciding that even if you screw up, even if you fail, you'll be further ahead than if you stayed stuck in neutral. Because here's the thing: no one's coming to push you. You've got to push yourself.

The hardest part of anything is the beginning. It's staring at the blank page, lacing up your running shoes, picking up the phone, or opening the door to the gym. Once you start, momentum takes over. But getting started? That takes guts. And it takes a willingness to be bad at something before you get good at it.

Here's the secret: you don't have to start big. In fact, you shouldn't. Big, sweeping changes are intimidating and unsustainable. Start small. Pick the tiniest possible action you can take right now and do it. Want to start working out? Do ten push-ups. Want to write a book? Write one crappy sentence. Want to start a business? Google how to register an LLC. The point isn't to do it all at once; the point is to start. Because starting creates momentum, and momentum is everything.

But here's the kicker: starting doesn't feel good. It's awkward and uncomfortable, and you'll probably suck at first. That's normal. Everyone sucks at the beginning. Michael Jordan wasn't born sinking free throws. Picasso's first paintings probably looked like a toddler's finger art. The only difference between them and the people who gave up is that they kept going. They didn't let the discomfort of starting stop them. And neither should you.

The biggest lie you tell yourself is, "I'll start tomorrow." Tomorrow is the graveyard of dreams. It's where good intentions go to die. If you're serious about changing your life, tomorrow isn't an option. Today is the only time you have. So, stop waiting for some magical day when you feel ready or motivated. It's not coming. The only way to feel ready is to start before you are.

Starting isn't glamorous. No one's going to applaud you for taking the first step. Hell, most people won't even notice. But that's okay. This isn't about them; it's about you. It's about proving to yourself that you're not the kind of person who sits around waiting for life to happen. You're the kind of person who makes things happen. And that starts with one small, imperfect step.

Let me save you some time: the first step isn't going to be pretty. You're going to mess up. You're going to second-guess yourself. And you're going to wonder if you're wasting your time. But here's the thing: the first step doesn't have to be perfect.

It just has to be done. Perfection is the enemy of progress, and waiting until you're "perfect" is just another excuse to do nothing.

Here's a trick: when you don't know what to do, just pick something. Anything. Even if it's the wrong move, it's better than no move. Action creates clarity. Sitting around thinking about what to do next doesn't. You can't steer a parked car, and you can't course-correct if you're not moving. So, start. Screw it up if you have to, but start.

And stop talking about it. Stop telling everyone what you're *going* to do. No one cares about your plans—they care about your results. Talking about your goals feels good because it gives you a hit of validation, but it doesn't get you any closer to achieving them. So, shut up about what you're going to do and use that energy to actually do it.

At the end of the day, starting is a choice. It's not about waiting for the perfect conditions, the perfect plan, or the perfect time. It's about deciding that you're done waiting. It's about taking the leap, even if you're scared, even if you're not sure what comes next. Because the alternative is staying exactly where you are—and you deserve better than that.

So, what are you waiting for? Shut up, stop overthinking, and get started. Right now. Not tomorrow. Not later. Now. Because the only way to get where you want to go is to take the first step. And once you do, you'll realize it was never as hard as you made it out to be.

Chapter 9: Procrastination: The Art of Screwing Yourself Over

Let's talk about procrastination. The sneaky little devil that convinces you it's okay to wait until later to do what you should be doing now. It's seductive, isn't it? It whispers in your ear, "Just five more minutes of scrolling," or "You'll be way more productive if you start tomorrow." And before you know it, five minutes turns into five hours, and tomorrow turns into never.

Procrastination isn't laziness. It's sabotage. It's you, standing in your own way, inventing distractions to avoid the discomfort of doing the work. It's not about time management—it's about fear. Fear of failing, fear of not being good enough, fear of facing something hard. Procrastination is fear in sheep's clothing, and if you don't get it under control, it will quietly ruin your life.

Here's the thing about procrastination: it feels harmless in the moment. You tell yourself you'll do it later, and it doesn't feel like a big deal. But every time you put something off, you're making a choice. You're choosing comfort over progress, short-term pleasure over long-term success. And those little choices? They add up. They compound, until one day you wake up and realize you've wasted years on distractions and empty promises to yourself.

The worst part? Procrastination is sneaky. It doesn't always look like wasting time. Sometimes it looks like being busy. You convince yourself that organizing your desk, cleaning the house, or catching up on emails is productive, but deep down, you know it's just another way to avoid the real work. It's a guilt-free way to procrastinate, but it's still procrastination.

You've probably heard the saying, "If it's important, you'll find a way. If it's not, you'll find an excuse." Well, procrastination is the master of excuses. It's the voice in your head that tells you you're too tired, too busy, or too distracted to start right now. And the longer you listen to it, the stronger it gets. Procrastination is like a muscle—the more you use it, the better you get at avoiding the hard stuff.

So, how do you break the cycle? You start by calling it out. Be brutally honest with yourself. The next time you catch yourself procrastinating, stop and ask, "What am I avoiding right now?" Nine times out of ten, the thing you're avoiding is the thing you need to do most. And the only way to deal with it is to face it head-on.

Here's the secret: action kills procrastination. It doesn't have to be big action—just something to break the inertia. The hardest part is starting, but once you do, momentum takes over. It's like pushing a car—it's tough to get it moving, but once it's rolling, it's much easier to keep it going. So, take the smallest possible step. Write one sentence. Do one push-up. Make one phone call. Just start.

And stop waiting for motivation. Motivation is a fair-weather friend. It shows up when things are easy but disappears the second things get tough. Discipline, on the other hand, doesn't care how you feel. Discipline gets up and works, even when you'd rather be doing anything else. So, forget about waiting to feel inspired. Do the work, and let motivation catch up to you later.

Another trick? Set a timer. Give yourself 10 minutes to focus on the task you've been avoiding. Tell yourself you can quit after 10 minutes if you really want to. Most of the time, you'll find that once you've started, you'll keep going. The hardest part is getting over the initial hump, and a timer makes it easier to take that first step.

But let's be real: breaking the habit of procrastination isn't easy. It takes practice. It takes self-awareness. And it takes a willingness to sit with discomfort. Because that's what procrastination is really about—avoiding discomfort. The discomfort of hard work, of uncertainty, of doing something that might not go perfectly. But here's the thing: growth is uncomfortable. Progress is uncomfortable. And if you want to achieve anything worthwhile, you've got to get comfortable with being uncomfortable.

So, the next time you feel the urge to procrastinate, stop and ask yourself this: "What's the cost of waiting?" Because every time you put something off, you're robbing your future self of time, opportunities, and progress. You're choosing to stay stuck, to stay small, to stay exactly where you are. And for what? A few more minutes of scrolling? Another rerun of a show you've already seen? It's not worth it.

At the end of the day, procrastination is a choice. You can choose to wait, or you can choose to act. You can choose comfort, or you can choose growth. And while it might feel good to procrastinate in the moment, the regret of wasted time will haunt you far longer than the discomfort of doing the work ever will.

So, stop screwing yourself over. Stop making excuses. And for the love of all that's productive, stop waiting for the perfect moment. It doesn't exist. The only moment you have is now. Use it wisely.

Chapter 10: Confidence Is Earned, Not Gifted

Confidence. It's the thing everyone wants but few truly understand. We idolize confident people—the ones who seem so sure of themselves, who walk into a room like they own it, who tackle challenges without hesitation. And somewhere along the way, we convinced ourselves that confidence is an inherent trait. Something you're born with, like eye color or height. But here's the truth no one tells you: confidence isn't gifted. It's earned.

You don't wake up one day suddenly full of confidence. You build it. You earn it through action, through showing up, through proving to yourself over and over again that you can handle whatever life throws at you. Confidence isn't something someone else can give you—it's a reward for doing the work, taking the risks, and showing up for yourself.

But here's the catch: most people are waiting for confidence to show up first. They think, "I'll take the leap when I feel more confident," or "I'll go after my goals when I'm sure I won't fail." That's backward. Confidence doesn't come before action—it comes after. You don't feel confident and then act; you act and then feel confident because you've proven to yourself that you can do it.

Think of confidence like a muscle. It doesn't grow by sitting around wishing it were stronger. It grows by being used, stretched, and challenged. Every time you step out of your comfort zone, every time you try something new, every time you push yourself to do the thing that scares you, you're strengthening that muscle. It's not always pretty, and it's definitely not always comfortable, but that's the only way to build it.

Here's the thing: confidence is built on evidence. You don't just tell yourself you're capable—you show yourself. You collect little victories, one after another, until you can't deny your own competence. It starts small. You show up to the gym on the days you don't feel like it. You speak up in meetings even when your voice shakes. You make the phone call you've been dreading. Each of these moments might seem insignificant on their own, but together, they add up to something powerful. They become proof. Proof that you can do hard things, that you can face challenges, and that you can trust yourself to follow through.

But let's be real: building confidence isn't fun at first. It feels awkward and uncomfortable. You're going to fail. You're going to doubt yourself. You're going to have moments where you feel like a fraud. And that's okay. Confidence doesn't mean never feeling fear or doubt—it means acting despite them. It means showing up for yourself, even when you don't feel 100% ready.

The problem is, too many people let their lack of confidence stop them from trying. They think, "What if I fail? What if I embarrass myself? What if I'm not good enough?" But here's the harsh reality: failure, embarrassment, and self-doubt are part of the process. You don't build confidence by avoiding them—you build it by facing them head-on. Confidence isn't the absence of fear; it's the willingness to act in spite of it.

Another truth about confidence? It's not a one-time achievement. You don't reach a certain level and stay there forever. Confidence is fluid. It grows and fades depending on your actions. If you stop challenging yourself, if you stop pushing your boundaries, your confidence will shrink. That's why you've got to keep showing up, keep proving to yourself that you can handle more than you think.

And let's talk about fake confidence for a second—the kind that's all show and no substance. You've seen it before: the loud, cocky types who talk a big game but crumble under pressure. That's not confidence. That's insecurity in a flashy coat. True confidence is quiet. It doesn't need to prove itself to anyone because it's built on a solid foundation of action and self-trust. It's not about being the loudest in the room; it's about knowing, deep down, that you can handle whatever comes your way.

So, how do you start building real confidence? You start by keeping your promises—to others, sure, but more importantly, to yourself. When you say you're going to do something, do it. When you commit to a goal, follow through. Every time you keep a promise to yourself, you're building trust. And trust is the foundation of confidence.

You also have to stop comparing your chapter one to someone else's chapter twenty. Confidence isn't about being the best—it's about being better than you were yesterday. Focus on your own progress, your own growth, and your own journey.

Because the truth is, no one else's opinion of you matters nearly as much as your own. Confidence isn't about convincing the world you're capable; it's about convincing yourself.

At the end of the day, confidence isn't some magical gift that a lucky few are born with. It's not a feeling that just shows up one day. It's something you earn through action, through persistence, through showing up for yourself even when it's hard. It's built step by step, day by day, until one day you look back and realize you've become the kind of person you always wanted to be.

So, stop waiting to feel confident. Stop telling yourself you're not ready. Start taking action, no matter how small, and let confidence catch up to you along the way. Because confidence isn't about feeling ready—it's about proving to yourself that you can do it anyway. And the best part? Once you've earned it, no one can take it away from you.

Chapter 11: When You're Tired, Keep Going

Let me guess—you're tired. You're worn out. You've had a long day, week, maybe even a long year, and you're thinking, *I deserve a break.* You're telling yourself that you've done enough, that it's okay to quit for now, that you'll pick it back up tomorrow. Sound familiar? Good. Let's talk about how that mindset is the exact reason you're stuck where you are.

Tired? Boo-freaking-hoo. You think you're the only one? Newsflash: everyone's tired. The difference is that the people who succeed don't let being tired stop them. They don't stop when they're tired; they stop when they're done. You, on the other hand, are using exhaustion as a crutch. You're letting it be the excuse that lets you off the hook. "Oh, I'm so tired, I'll just start fresh tomorrow." That's a lie, and you know it. Tomorrow turns into the next day, and the next, and before you know it, you've done nothing for weeks.

Here's the thing about tiredness: it's temporary. It's a feeling. And feelings don't have to dictate your actions unless you let them. You can be tired and still get the work done. You can be exhausted and still push through. It's not about how you feel; it's about what you do. The grind doesn't care that you're tired. Your goals don't care. Success doesn't care. The only thing that cares is the part of you looking for an excuse to quit.

Do you think the greats—people like Kobe Bryant, Elon Musk, or Oprah—got to where they are by giving up when they were tired? Hell no. Kobe was in the gym before the sun came up, after games, after everyone else had gone home. Elon Musk worked 100-hour weeks to get Tesla and SpaceX off the ground. Oprah didn't become a billionaire by taking naps every time she felt a little drained. They were tired. They were beyond tired. But they kept going because they understood something you apparently don't: no one gives a shit about how hard it is for you. The results are all that matter.

Here's a tough pill to swallow: your life right now is a direct result of what you've chosen to tolerate. If you're stuck, it's because you've let yourself settle. You've let your excuses win. You've decided that your comfort is more important than your progress. And let me tell you, that's pathetic. You can do better. You *know* you can do better. But instead of pushing through, you're sitting there, whining about how hard it is, as if that's going to change anything.

Being tired doesn't make you special. It doesn't make you a victim. It makes you human. The question isn't whether you're tired—it's whether you're willing to push past it. Because if you're not, guess what? Someone else will. Someone else will outwork you, outlast you, and take the opportunities you were too weak to grab. And when that happens, you'll have no one to blame but yourself.

Now, I'm not saying burnout isn't real. It is. But let's not confuse burnout with basic fatigue. Burnout happens after months or years of relentless pressure with no breaks, no boundaries, and no balance. What you're feeling right now? That's just tired. It's the kind of tired you feel after a tough workout, a long day, or a string of late nights. It's the kind of tired you can push through, and you know it.

And let's be honest: half the time you're not even physically tired. You're mentally tired. You've been scrolling on your phone, binge-watching Netflix, or wasting time on things that don't matter, and now you're mentally drained from overstimulation. That's not real tiredness. That's self-inflicted bullshit. If you spent half as much time actually working on your goals as you do finding ways to avoid them, you'd be a hell of a lot further along by now.

So here's what you're going to do: you're going to stop whining. You're going to stop telling yourself that you'll do it tomorrow or next week or whenever you feel more energized. You're going to get up, right now, and take one step forward. I don't care how small that step is—just take it. Write one sentence. Make one call. Do one thing. And then do the next thing, and the next. Momentum doesn't come from resting; it comes from moving.

And let me be crystal clear: if you're not willing to push through the discomfort, you don't deserve the reward. Success isn't free, and it's not handed out to people who quit every time they feel a little tired. If you want it, you've got to earn it. You've got to show up when it's hard. You've got to keep going when you don't want to. That's what separates the winners from the losers. That's what separates you from the life you could be living.

So, what's it going to be? Are you going to keep making excuses, keep choosing comfort over progress, keep settling for less than you're capable of? Or are you going to get off your ass, push through the tiredness, and prove to yourself that you're stronger than your excuses?

Because here's the truth: no one's coming to save you. No one's going to give you a break, a handout, or a shortcut. It's just you, your goals, and the work. So, stop wasting time. Stop feeling sorry for yourself. When you're tired, keep going. Because that's where greatness lives—on the other side of your excuses.

Chapter 12: Be the Most Reliable Person You Know

Let's talk about reliability—one of the most underrated and least glamorous keys to success. Being reliable isn't flashy, and it doesn't get a lot of attention, but it's the foundation of everything that matters in life. You can have all the talent in the world, but if people can't count on you, you're useless. Harsh? Maybe. True? Absolutely.

Here's the deal: being reliable means doing what you say you're going to do, when you say you're going to do it, no matter how you feel or what obstacles pop up. It means showing up consistently—not just when it's convenient or when you're in the mood. If that sounds boring, good. Reliability isn't supposed to be exciting. It's supposed to work.

Now let me ask you something: are you reliable? And don't just answer with a knee-jerk "yes." Really think about it. Can the people around you count on you? Can *you* count on you? Because if you're the type of person who makes promises you can't keep, who overcommits and underdelivers, or who flakes out the second something gets hard, you're not reliable—you're a liability. And that needs to change. Fast.

Being unreliable is the quickest way to lose respect, trust, and opportunities. It's also one of the easiest bad habits to fix—if you're willing to stop making excuses and start taking responsibility. Because here's the thing: reliability isn't about talent, intelligence, or luck. It's about effort. It's about deciding that your word means something and backing it up with action.

Let's be real—most people suck at this. They say yes to things they have no intention of following through on. They cancel plans at the last minute. They miss deadlines and then come up with excuses like, "I got busy," or "Something came up." You know what that tells the world? That you're not serious. That you can't be trusted. That you're all talk and no action. And if that's the reputation you're building, good luck getting anyone to take you seriously.

Reliability isn't just about showing up for other people, though. It's about showing up for yourself. If you can't keep promises to yourself, how the hell are you going to keep them to anyone else?

Every time you tell yourself you're going to do something—whether it's starting a project, hitting the gym, or saving money—and then you don't, you're teaching yourself that your word doesn't mean anything. And that's a recipe for failure.

Here's a simple truth: reliable people win. They don't always win the fastest, and they don't always make the most noise, but they win in the long run. Why? Because people trust them. Employers trust them. Friends trust them. Clients trust them. And trust is currency. It's the most valuable thing you can earn in any relationship, personal or professional. If you're reliable, people will want to work with you, support you, and bet on you. If you're not, they won't.

Being reliable isn't complicated, but it's not easy, either. It requires consistency, discipline, and a willingness to do the boring, unglamorous work of following through. It means showing up on time, meeting deadlines, and keeping your promises—even when it's inconvenient, even when you're tired, even when no one's watching. Especially when no one's watching.

And here's the kicker: reliability doesn't mean being perfect. It means being accountable. Everyone screws up sometimes. Deadlines get missed. Promises get broken. Life happens. The difference between a reliable person and an unreliable one is how they handle it. Reliable people own their mistakes, make it right, and do better next time. Unreliable people make excuses, shift blame, and repeat the same patterns. Which one do you want to be?

If you want to become the most reliable person you know, start small. Don't overcommit. Don't say yes to things you can't realistically deliver on. Underpromise and overdeliver. Build a reputation for being the person who always follows through, no matter what. And when you screw up—and you will—own it. Apologize, fix it, and make damn sure it doesn't happen again.

Here's the bottom line: reliability is a choice. It's not about your circumstances, your resources, or your talent. It's about deciding that you're going to show up, do the work, and keep your word—every single time. It's about being the kind of person people can count on, no matter what.

So, stop flaking. Stop making excuses. Stop being the person who talks big and delivers small. Be the most reliable person you know. Be the person who gets shit done, no matter what. Because in a world full of people who can't be counted on, being reliable isn't just an advantage—it's a superpower.

Chapter 13: Why "Balance" Is Bullshit

Let's get this out of the way: balance is a myth. The idea that you can have it all—work-life harmony, perfect relationships, thriving careers, all while meditating and drinking your green smoothie every morning—is total bullshit. Balance isn't just overrated; it's a fantasy sold to you by people who want you to think they've got life figured out. Newsflash: they don't.

Here's the truth no one tells you: doing anything worthwhile requires imbalance. It requires sacrifice, obsession, and a willingness to prioritize what matters most, even if it means letting other things slide. You can't chase big goals and expect everything in your life to stay perfectly aligned. That's not how success works. It's messy. It's chaotic. It's uncomfortable. And that's okay.

The people preaching balance are the same ones telling you to "listen to your body" when you're tired, or "take it easy" when things get tough. But guess what? That's not how you win. You don't win by splitting your energy equally across everything in your life. You win by going all-in on the things that matter and accepting that other areas are going to take a hit for a while. Balance is for people who are content to coast. Imbalance is for people who want to dominate.

Think about anyone who's achieved greatness. Do you think they had balance? Do you think Serena Williams worried about work-life harmony when she was training to become one of the greatest athletes in history? Do you think Steve Jobs was concerned about "unplugging" while he was building Apple? Hell no. They were obsessed. They were unbalanced. They poured everything they had into their goals, and that's why they succeeded.

Now, don't get me wrong. I'm not saying you should ignore your health, your family, or your relationships. Those things matter. But let's be real: there are seasons in life where balance simply isn't an option. If you're building a business, launching a new project, or chasing a dream, you're going to have to sacrifice some "balance" to make it happen. That's just the reality.

Here's where most people screw up: they treat balance as an excuse to avoid discomfort. "I don't want to burn out," they say. "I need balance." Translation: "I'm not willing to work hard enough to succeed." Balance becomes a crutch, a way to justify half-assing their efforts and staying in their comfort zone. Don't fall for that trap. Burnout doesn't come from working hard. It comes from working hard on things you don't care about. If you're passionate about what you're doing, imbalance isn't burnout—it's focus.

The problem with balance is that it's static. It assumes that every part of your life should get equal attention at all times, which is completely unrealistic. Life isn't static—it's dynamic. It's always changing. Some seasons require you to go all-in on work. Others require you to focus on family or health. The key isn't balance; it's alignment. Are your priorities aligned with your goals? Are you putting your energy into the things that matter most right now? If the answer is yes, then screw balance.

Of course, people will judge you for this. They'll say you're "too focused" or "too obsessed." They'll tell you to "relax" or "take it easy." Ignore them. These are the same people who will be stuck in the same place five years from now, still wondering why their dreams never materialized. You don't owe anyone an explanation for why you're going all-in. Let your results do the talking.

Here's the thing: balance is about maintaining the status quo. Imbalance is about growth. If you're constantly trying to balance everything, you're never going to move forward. You're just going to stay exactly where you are, juggling all the same shit, wondering why nothing's changing. Growth requires imbalance. It requires putting more energy into the things that matter and less energy into the things that don't.

Does this mean you'll have to make sacrifices? Yes. You might miss some family dinners, lose a little sleep, or skip a few nights out with your friends. But those sacrifices are temporary. The rewards, on the other hand, are permanent. The imbalance you create now is what allows you to build the life you want later.

At the end of the day, balance is a choice. You can choose to spread yourself thin, trying to keep everyone happy and maintain some illusion of harmony. Or you can choose to go all-in, accept the chaos, and focus on what really matters. One choice keeps you comfortable. The other takes you to the next level.

So, stop chasing balance. Stop trying to keep every part of your life perfectly aligned. Start chasing alignment instead. Focus on what matters most. Embrace the imbalance. And when people tell you to "slow down" or "find balance," smile, nod, and get back to work. Because while they're busy juggling, you'll be busy winning.

Chapter 14: Work Now, Rest Later (Or Never)

Let's talk about rest. The thing everyone's obsessed with these days. Everywhere you turn, someone's telling you to slow down, practice self-care, take a day off. Look, I get it—burnout is real, and nobody's saying you should work yourself into the ground for no reason. But let's be honest: the rest crowd has gotten out of control. Rest has become the go-to excuse for people who don't want to do the hard stuff.

You know who tells you to "rest more"? People who aren't doing anything worth getting tired over. They're preaching balance and recovery while staying in the exact same place year after year. They say, "Work smarter, not harder," and then proceed to do neither. Meanwhile, the people out there crushing it? They're working their asses off. They're grinding while everyone else is taking naps and posting about how "rest is resistance." Please. Rest isn't resistance—it's surrender.

Here's the reality: if you want something bad enough, there will be seasons where rest isn't an option. Success demands sacrifice. It demands late nights, early mornings, and a level of effort most people aren't willing to give. That's why most people aren't successful. They're too busy protecting their "downtime" to make any real progress.

I'm not saying you should never rest. I'm saying you need to earn it. Rest isn't a right; it's a reward. You don't get to kick your feet up just because you're tired. You get to rest when the work is done, not a second before. And if you're serious about your goals, the work is never really done. There's always another level, another milestone, another way to push yourself further. So, ask yourself this: are you resting because you've earned it, or because you're looking for an excuse to quit?

You want to know why so many people stay stuck? Because they rest too damn much. They take breaks before they've built any momentum. They start something, get tired, and decide it's time for "self-care." Here's a newsflash: self-care isn't bubble baths and Netflix binges. Self-care is doing the hard things now so your future self can have a life worth living. It's about investing in yourself, not coddling yourself. Sometimes, the best self-care is putting your head down and doing the work.

Think about it: the people who succeed don't have more hours in the day than you. They don't have magical energy reserves or superhuman abilities. They just have a different mindset. They don't see tiredness as a reason to stop; they see it as a challenge to overcome. They know the real rewards come to those who push past the point where everyone else quits.

Here's the truth: rest is addictive. The more you rest, the more you want to rest. It's like quicksand—easy to fall into and hard to get out of. One lazy day turns into a lazy week, and before you know it, you've lost all the momentum you worked so hard to build. And the worst part? You convince yourself you needed it. You tell yourself you were "burnt out" or "taking care of yourself," but deep down, you know the truth: you just didn't want to do the work.

Let me make this clear: burnout isn't the result of working hard. It's the result of working hard on the wrong things—or not seeing progress on the things that matter. If you're grinding day and night and getting nowhere, yeah, you'll burn out. But if you're grinding and seeing results, the work energizes you. It fuels you. It makes the sacrifices worth it. So instead of worrying about burnout, worry about whether you're putting your energy into the right places. If you are, the grind won't break you—it'll make you stronger.

Now, let's talk about what happens when you finally do rest. You've worked your ass off, hit a milestone, and decide it's time for a break. That's fine. You've earned it. But don't let a short break turn into a long one. Rest is a pit stop, not a parking lot. Too many people hit one goal, take their foot off the gas, and never get back up to speed. Don't let that be you. Rest when you need to, but always keep your eyes on the next goal. Success doesn't take vacations, and neither should you.

And let's get real for a second: sometimes, you don't need rest—you need to toughen up. Life is hard. Work is hard. Chasing your dreams is hard. That's the price of admission. If you're constantly looking for ways to avoid the discomfort, you'll never make it. The people at the top aren't there because it was easy. They're there because they pushed through the hard parts while everyone else quit. They kept working when they were tired, frustrated, and overwhelmed. They didn't stop because they knew the work was worth it.

So, what's your excuse? Are you tired? Good. That means you're doing something. Are you overwhelmed? Great. That means you're stretching yourself. Are you uncomfortable? Perfect. That's where growth happens. Stop seeing these things as problems and start seeing them as proof that you're on the right track.

At the end of the day, rest is a choice. You can choose to rest now and stay where you are, or you can choose to work now and rest later—when you've actually earned it. The question is, how bad do you want it? Because if you're serious about your goals, you'll stop looking for reasons to rest and start looking for ways to keep going.

Work now, rest later—or never. The choice is yours. But don't sit there whining about how hard it is and expect anyone to feel sorry for you. The grind doesn't care about your feelings. The work doesn't care that you're tired. Success doesn't care about your excuses. So, get up. Get moving. And keep going until you've earned the right to rest. And when you do? Rest quickly. Because the next level is waiting.

Chapter 15: You're the Problem, But You're Also the Solution

It's time to face a harsh truth: if your life isn't where you want it to be, there's only one person to blame—you. Yeah, I said it. You. Not your boss, not your parents, not the economy, and definitely not Mercury being in retrograde. You are the common denominator in all of your problems. And until you accept that, you'll stay stuck right where you are.

Let me guess, that stings a little. Good. It's supposed to. Growth doesn't happen in your comfort zone, and facing the fact that you're the problem is about as uncomfortable as it gets. But here's the good news: if you're the problem, then you're also the solution. The power to fix your life is—and always has been—entirely in your hands. That's the beauty of owning your shit.

Most people are experts at deflecting responsibility. They blame their circumstances, their upbringing, or their bad luck. "I can't get ahead because my boss doesn't like me." "I could've gone further if I had the right opportunities." "It's just not the right time for me." Blah, blah, blah. It's all bullshit. These excuses are nothing more than a way to protect your fragile ego from admitting that you're the reason you're not succeeding.

Here's a reality check: life doesn't owe you anything. No one's going to swoop in and fix your problems for you. No one's going to hand you the perfect job, the perfect relationship, or the perfect life. If you want something, you have to go out and get it. Period. Full stop. And that starts with taking responsibility for where you are right now.

You can't fix a problem you won't admit exists. If you're broke, stop blaming your low-paying job and start looking at how you're managing your money. If you're out of shape, stop blaming your busy schedule and start prioritizing your health. If your relationships suck, stop blaming everyone else and start working on yourself. Own it. All of it. Because until you do, nothing will change.

Let me be clear: taking responsibility isn't about beating yourself up or wallowing in guilt. It's about empowerment. It's about recognizing that you have the power to change your circumstances. If your life is a mess, guess what?

You have the ability to clean it up. If you're stuck, you have the ability to get unstuck. But that only happens when you stop pointing fingers and start looking in the mirror.

Here's the thing: taking responsibility isn't easy. It requires brutal honesty, self-awareness, and a willingness to face your flaws. It's not fun to admit that you've been lazy, undisciplined, or scared. It's not fun to realize that you've been standing in your own way. But until you do, you'll keep making the same mistakes, over and over, wondering why nothing ever changes.

Think of your life like a car. If you keep driving it into ditches, you can't blame the road, the weather, or the car itself. You're the driver. You're the one behind the wheel. And if you want to get to a better destination, you've got to take control of the damn steering wheel. That means making better choices, taking smarter actions, and being accountable for where you're headed.

Taking responsibility doesn't mean you have to do it all at once. Start small. Pick one area of your life that isn't working and ask yourself, "What can I do to fix this?" Not what your boss, your partner, or the universe can do—what *you* can do. And then do it. Take action, no matter how small, and keep taking action until things start to improve.

But don't just stop at action—take responsibility for your mindset, too. The way you think about your problems matters. If you see yourself as a victim of circumstance, you'll stay a victim. But if you see yourself as the solution, you'll find a way to overcome anything. Your thoughts shape your reality, so stop feeding yourself negative, self-pitying crap and start thinking like a problem-solver.

This isn't about perfection. You're going to screw up. You're going to make mistakes. And that's fine. What matters is how you respond. Do you own your failures and learn from them, or do you make excuses and stay stuck? Successful people aren't perfect—they're just relentless about taking responsibility, learning from their mistakes, and moving forward.

At the end of the day, your life is exactly what you've made it. If it's not where you want it to be, the only way to change it is to change yourself. That's not me being harsh—it's me being honest. No one's coming to save you, but the good news is, you don't need anyone to. You're perfectly capable of saving yourself. You just have to stop waiting for someone else to fix your problems and start doing the work.

So, stop being the problem and start being the solution. Take ownership of your life, take action, and stop making excuses. Because the truth is, everything you want is on the other side of responsibility. The question is, are you willing to step up and take it? Or are you going to keep getting in your own way? The choice is yours.

Chapter 16: Cut the Crap and Commit

Here's the thing about commitment: most people are terrible at it. They dip their toes into the water but never dive in. They're "interested" in success, but they're not committed to it. They like the idea of achieving their goals, but when it comes time to put in the work? They waffle. They hesitate. They quit. And then they wonder why nothing in their life ever changes.

Let me be blunt: you can't half-ass your way to success. You can't kind of want it. You can't be sort of committed. If you're not all in, you're wasting your time. Commitment isn't a feeling; it's a decision. It's deciding that you're going to do whatever it takes, no matter how hard it gets, no matter how long it takes, no matter how many obstacles you face. Period.

The problem is, most people don't want to commit because commitment is scary. It means taking responsibility. It means putting your ass on the line. It means risking failure, rejection, and discomfort. So instead, they dabble. They put one foot in and keep the other one firmly planted in their comfort zone. They tell themselves, "I'll try this for a while and see how it goes." That's not commitment. That's playing pretend.

You want to know why people fail? Because they quit at the first sign of difficulty. They hit a roadblock and think, *Maybe this isn't for me*. They face rejection and decide, *It's not worth it*. Here's a newsflash: commitment means not quitting. Ever. Not when it gets hard. Not when you're tired. Not when you feel like you're not making progress. Commitment means staying the course, no matter what. It means being relentless.

Think about the last time you set a goal for yourself. Did you actually commit to it? Or did you kind of, sort of want it? Did you tell yourself, "This is my priority, and I'm going to do whatever it takes," or did you tell yourself, "I'll give it a shot and see how I feel"? Be honest. Because if you weren't fully committed, you never really gave yourself a chance to succeed.

Here's the truth: commitment isn't glamorous. It's not exciting. It's not Instagram-worthy. Commitment is waking up early when you want to sleep in. It's saying no to distractions, temptations, and excuses. It's doing the work, day after day, even when it feels like you're not making progress. Commitment is boring. It's unsexy. But it's also the only thing that works.

And let's get one thing straight: commitment isn't just about starting strong. It's about staying strong. Anyone can be excited at the beginning of a new goal. The real test is whether you can keep going when the excitement wears off. Because it will wear off. The grind will get tough. The obstacles will pile up. And that's where most people throw in the towel. But not you. Not if you're truly committed.

Let me tell you what commitment looks like: it looks like showing up when no one else does. It looks like giving 100% effort even when you feel like crap. It looks like staying focused when everyone around you is distracted. Commitment isn't flashy, but it's powerful. It's the thing that keeps you moving forward when everything else tells you to quit.

The truth is, you're probably more capable than you think. But you'll never know until you commit. Half-assing your efforts only gives you half-assed results. If you want to see what you're really made of, you've got to go all in. You've got to burn the boats. You've got to eliminate "maybe" from your vocabulary and replace it with "hell yes."

Commitment doesn't mean you won't fail. You will. It doesn't mean you won't face setbacks. You will. It doesn't mean it won't suck sometimes. It will. But commitment means getting back up every single time. It means refusing to let failure stop you. It means being so damn stubborn that the world eventually has no choice but to give you what you want.

So, how do you commit? You start by deciding what you really want. Not what sounds nice. Not what other people expect of you. What *you* truly want. Once you've decided, cut the crap. Stop making excuses. Stop waiting for the perfect time. Stop hedging your bets. Go all in. Burn the boats. Make it so there's no way out but forward.

And here's the thing about commitment: it's contagious. Once you fully commit to one area of your life, you'll start to see how it transforms everything else. Committing to your goals will make you a stronger, more disciplined, more resilient person. It'll show you what you're capable of. And that confidence will spill over into everything you do.

At the end of the day, commitment is a choice. You can choose to dabble, to play it safe, to stay on the sidelines. Or you can choose to go all in, to embrace the grind, to be relentless in the pursuit of your goals. The question is, how bad do you want it? Because if you're not willing to fully commit, you don't want it bad enough.

So, stop pretending. Stop waffling. Cut the crap and commit. Right now. Not tomorrow, not next week, not when you "feel ready." Do it now. And when it gets hard—and it will—remember this: commitment isn't about how you feel. It's about what you've decided. So decide. And then follow through. All the way. No matter what.

Chapter 17: How to Stop Caring About Everyone Else's Opinion

Here's the hard truth: most of the things holding you back have nothing to do with your abilities, resources, or circumstances. They have to do with your obsession with what other people think. You're stuck because you care too damn much about how you'll look, what people will say, and whether or not you'll be judged. And let me tell you: caring about everyone else's opinion is a one-way ticket to mediocrity.

You can't please everyone, so stop trying. The second you start chasing other people's approval, you lose control of your life. You let their opinions dictate your actions. You let their judgments paralyze you. And for what? So you can stay small, stay safe, and avoid rocking the boat? Congratulations, you're officially living your life for other people.

You know what's worse than failure? Regret. Regret that you wasted your time worrying about what people thought instead of going after what you wanted. Regret that you kept your mouth shut because you were afraid of being laughed at. Regret that you let someone else's irrelevant opinion keep you from living the life you deserve. And here's the kicker: most of the people whose opinions you're worried about? They're not even thinking about you. They're too busy worrying about their own lives to care about yours.

But let's be real: it's not easy to stop caring. We're wired to seek approval. It's human nature to want to fit in, to be liked, to avoid rejection. But here's what you need to understand: other people's opinions aren't facts. They're not the ultimate truth. They're just noise. And if you spend your life trying to tune into every frequency, you'll never hear your own voice.

Think about the people whose opinions you're so worried about. Do they matter? Are they living the kind of life you aspire to? Have they done the things you want to do? Or are they just projecting their own fears and insecurities onto you? Because most of the time, people's judgments say more about them than they do about you. Their opinions are a reflection of their limitations, not yours.

And let's not forget the haters—the people who go out of their way to tear you down. Here's the secret to dealing with them: they don't matter. Haters don't hate you; they hate themselves. They hate that you're doing something they're too scared to do. They hate that you're willing to take risks while they sit on the sidelines. So they project their bitterness onto you. Don't take it personally. Pity them if you must, but don't let their negativity slow you down.

Here's the truth: the people who matter—the ones who truly care about you—will support you no matter what. They might not always understand your goals or agree with your choices, but they'll respect your willingness to go after what you want. And if they don't? That's on them, not you. Your job isn't to live for other people's approval; it's to live for yourself.

So, how do you stop caring about what people think? You start by getting clear on what you want. When you're laser-focused on your goals, other people's opinions become background noise. You don't have time to worry about what your coworker, neighbor, or random person on the internet thinks when you're busy chasing your dreams.

Next, you have to toughen up. Stop taking everything so personally. Not everyone is going to like you, and that's okay. If you're doing anything worthwhile, you're going to piss some people off. You're going to make people uncomfortable. That's part of the process. If everyone likes you, it's because you're not making any waves. And if you're not making waves, you're not making progress.

Another thing: stop looking for validation. You don't need permission to chase your goals. You don't need applause to know you're on the right track. Trust yourself. Trust your instincts. The only validation you need is your own. The second you stop seeking approval from others is the second you take your power back.

And here's the most liberating realization: no one's opinion can hurt you unless you let it. You have to give someone's words permission to matter, and you can revoke that permission anytime you want. Their opinions are powerless unless you hand them the keys to your self-worth. So stop handing them out like candy.

Here's a question for you: what would you do if no one was watching? If no one could judge you, criticize you, or question you? That's the life you should be living. That's the person you should be every day. Because at the end of the day, the only opinion that truly matters is your own. You're the one who has to live with your choices, your regrets, and your successes. Make them count.

So, stop caring about what everyone else thinks. Stop letting their opinions hold you back. Their approval isn't worth sacrificing your goals, your happiness, or your potential. Live boldly. Chase your dreams unapologetically. Let them judge, criticize, and doubt you. Let them watch as you prove them wrong. Because while they're busy talking, you'll be busy winning.

Chapter 18: Get Over Yourself and Get It Done

Let's pause for a moment. Take a deep breath. Seriously, do it. Inhale, exhale. This is the last chapter, and I want you to really sit with what I'm about to say. You've made it this far, and that says something. You've read the words, thought about the ideas, maybe even felt a spark of inspiration along the way. That's a start. But now I have to ask you: what are you going to do with it?

Because if you've read this entire book, nodded your head at the truths, and then go back to your same old habits, what was the point? What was the point of all the time you spent reading these chapters if you're just going to keep making the same excuses, keep letting fear win, keep putting off the life you know you're capable of living? If you walk away from this book unchanged, that's not on me. That's on you.

Here's the reality: nothing in this book will matter if you don't act on it. Nothing will matter if you close these pages, get up, and keep doing the same crap you've been doing all along. Reading isn't transformation. Thinking isn't transformation. Transformation happens when you get off your ass and change. And change is messy. It's uncomfortable. It's hard. But it's also worth it—if you have the guts to follow through.

You want the truth? Most people won't do it. Most people will read this book, feel a little motivated for a day or two, and then slide right back into the comfortable mediocrity they've been living in. They'll keep procrastinating, keep making excuses, and keep convincing themselves that "someday" they'll get around to it. Someday is a lie. Someday doesn't exist. If you're not willing to start now, you're wasting your time and mine.

I'm not here to pat you on the back for reading this far. I'm here to challenge you to do something about it. To get up and face the parts of yourself that you've been avoiding. To look at your fears, your failures, your flaws, and decide that they don't define you. To stop letting your past dictate your future. You are not a victim of your circumstances—you are the author of them. And it's time to start writing a better story.

The truth is, you've been the problem all along. You've been standing in your own way, sabotaging yourself, and blaming the world for your lack of progress. That's the bad news. But here's the good news: you're also the solution. You have the power to change your story, but only if you stop making excuses and start taking responsibility. Only if you stop waiting for someone to save you and start saving yourself.

No one is coming. No one's going to hand you the life you want. No one's going to do the work for you. And you know what? That's a gift. Because it means you don't have to wait for anyone. You don't have to depend on anyone. The power is yours, and it always has been.

But let's not sugarcoat it: if you don't act now, you're wasting time. Precious time. Time you don't get back. Every day you spend stuck in the same patterns is a day you're stealing from your future self. Think about that. Think about the version of you five years from now. Are they proud of the choices you're making today? Or are they pissed that you wasted so much time waiting, hesitating, and playing small?

This is your wake-up call. If you don't get serious about your goals now, when will you? If you don't face your fears now, when will you? If you don't start living the life you want now, then what the hell are you waiting for? The perfect moment? It doesn't exist. The right time? It's now. Always now.

You've got one life. One. And it's slipping away every second. That might sound dramatic, but it's the truth. You don't have time to waste worrying about what people think, doubting yourself, or waiting for motivation. You've already wasted enough. This is your moment. Right now. To decide whether you're going to step up and do the work or let another day, another month, another year pass you by.

So, here's my challenge to you: stop reading and start doing. Take everything you've learned from this book and put it into action. Not tomorrow. Not next week. Right now. Close this book and take one step toward the life you want. Just one step. And then take another. And another. Keep going until you're living a life that makes you proud.

This book was never about giving you answers. It was about pushing you to ask better questions. Questions like: What do I really want? What's holding me back? And most importantly, what am I going to do about it? If you can answer those questions honestly and act on them relentlessly, you don't need me or anyone else to tell you what to do. You already know.

Now it's time to stop thinking, stop waiting, and stop doubting. It's time to get over yourself and get it done. No excuses. No hesitation. Just action. Because the life you want isn't going to build itself. It's waiting for you to step up and make it happen.

So, what's it going to be? Are you going to put this book down and let it gather dust on a shelf? Or are you going to get up and make the changes you know you need to make? The choice is yours. Always has been. Always will be.

Don't waste it.

Get over yourself.

Get it done.

Personal Contract: My Commitment to Myself

This is it—the moment where I stop making excuses, stop waiting for the perfect time, and start taking responsibility for my life. I am done standing in my own way. From this moment forward, I commit to doing the hard, necessary, and uncomfortable work to become the person I know I'm capable of being.

I promise to:

1. **Take Responsibility**
   I will own my actions, my choices, and my results. No more blaming, no more excuses. My success or failure is on me, and I will face that truth every day.

2. **Act Despite Fear**
   Fear is no longer my excuse. I will move forward, even when I'm scared, even when I feel unprepared, because progress only happens outside my comfort zone.

3. **Show Up Every Day**
   Whether I feel motivated or not, whether it's easy or hard, I will show up and do the work. Discipline will guide me, not my fleeting feelings.

4. **Stop Seeking Approval**
   I will stop living for other people's opinions and start living for myself. My goals and values are my compass, and I will follow them unapologetically.

5. **Keep My Promises**
   When I make a commitment—whether to myself or others—I will follow through. My word will be my bond, and I will build trust in myself through action.

6. **Embrace the Grind**
   I understand that success isn't glamorous. It's messy, difficult, and requires sacrifice. I will lean into the grind, knowing it's the only path to what I want.

I understand that this contract is not a suggestion or a wish—it's a promise. A promise to myself, to my future, and to the life I want to build. From this moment on, I will take action. I will get over myself. And I will get it done.

Signed: _____

Date: _____

"The life you want is waiting—but only if you're willing to go get it."